Please renew/return items by last date
shown. Please call the number below:

Renewals and enquiries: 0300 1234049

Textphone for hearing or
speech impaired users: 01992 555506

www.hertfordshire.gov.uk/libraries
L32

Hertfordshire

What's in the
BIBLE?

An introduction to the
book of the Christian faith

Deborah Lock

LION
CHILDREN'S

Text by Deborah Lock based on text from *What is the Bible?* copyright © 2003 Sue Graves
This edition copyright © 2021 Lion Hudson IP Limited

Published by
Lion Hudson Limited
Prama House, 267 Banbury Road
Summertown, Oxford OX2 7HT, England
www.lionhudson.com

ISBN 978 0 7459 7966 3
First edition 2021

Acknowledgments

The publisher would like to thank Claire Clinton, Director of Religious Education and RSHE, RE Matters Ltd for consultancy advice.
Scriptures quotations are from the Good News Bible © 1994 published by the Bible Societies/HarperCollins Publishers Ltd UK, Good News Bible© American Bible Society 1966, 1971, 1976, 1992. Used with permission.

Picture acknowledgements

Every effort has been made to contact the illustrators of this work, although this has not been possible in all cases. If notified, the publisher will rectify any errors or omissions at the earliest opportunity.

Illustrations

Alan Parry: pp. 12, 16, 41; **Bill Corbett**: pp. 14(t), 19; **Carolyn Cox**: p. 30 (from *The Lion Children's Bible*); **Fred Apps**: p. 17; **Gail Newey**: p. 5; **Lion Hudson IP Ltd**: pp. 10, 14(b), 26; (John Williams) pp. 6 and back cover, 27, 29; (Chris Molan) p.25; **Martin Sanders**: pp. 13, 18, 23, 28(t), 34 (t) and back cover, 43; **Peter Dennis**: pp. 8, 15, 21, 24, 36; **Richard Scott**: pp. 1, 7, 20(t), 22, 31, 32, 33, 34(b), 35, 37, 38 and front cover, 45; **Steve Noon**: p. 11

Photographs

Chester Beatty Library: p. 9; **Hanan Isachar**: p. 3; **istock**: p. 40(t) (ke77kz); **Shutterstock**: pp. 4 (pixelheadphoto digitalskillet); 20(b) (Kovaleva_Ka); 28(b) (Pozdeyev Vitaly); 40(b) (Platslee); 42 (Jaime Pharr)

A catalogue record for this book is available from the British Library

Printed and bound in China, July 2021, LH54

CONTENTS

What is the BIBLE?

The Bible is the holy book of the **Christian faith**. The Bible tells about the God the Christians believe in, God's relationship with people, and how God's plans and purposes are completed through Jesus Christ. The Bible is a collection of books split into two parts: **The Old Testament** and **The New Testament**.

Christians often read the Bible a a family and tall about what the stories mean.

Christian faith

Christians believe in one God as Father, Son, and Holy Spirit. God the Father in heaven created the world and takes care of it. God the Son was born into the world as a human being, known as Jesus Christ. God the Holy Spirit is the power of God at work in the world. Christians find out more about God through reading the Bible.

The Old Testament

The roots of the Christian faith are found in the faith of the Jewish people. The ancient writings about the God of the Jewish people are found in the Hebrew Bible, also called the Tanakh. These writings have been rearranged into the first part of the Christian Bible called the Old Testament. Christians believe that these writings point the way to the coming of Jesus Christ. Jesus was born as a Jew and knew the special writings of his people. Christ means "chosen king".

The New Testament

The second part of the Christian Bible is called the New Testament. This tells about the life and teachings of Jesus Christ, and about his followers who went on to tell others about him. This includes letters written by some of the first Christians to new groups of followers, who had formed churches. This part was written in the 100 years after the life of Jesus.

Q: Did Jesus read the Bible?

In the New Testament there is a story about Jesus reading aloud from the scrolls of the Jewish special writings. It was the custom for all Jewish men to be invited to read from the scrolls. Jesus read these words written by the prophet Isaiah, afterwards saying that they were about himself:

The Spirit of the Lord is upon me, because he has chosen me to bring good news...
to set free the oppressed and announce that the time has come when the Lord will save his people.

Did you KNOW?

The word "Bible" is not used at all in the Bible. Instead the word "scriptures" is used to mean special holy writings.

Jesus reads from the scrolls.

What does "BIBLE" mean?

The word "Bible" comes from an ancient Greek word "biblia", which means books. The Christian Bible is a **collection** of over 60 different books, which were written for different reasons. The books would have first been written on **scrolls**. There are many different **types of writing** in the Bible.

Did you KNOW?

In 1947 ancient scrolls were found in caves by the Dead Sea. Many of the scrolls were parts of the Old Testament, and some dated from 400 BCE.

Collection of books

The books in the first part of the Bible record the history of the Jewish people and what they understood about God. The books tell about what happened to leaders and kings who were guided by or ignored God. Some are about people, known as prophets, who brought messages from God. The books in the second part help people to understand who Jesus was, what he said, and encourage his followers.

Ancient scrolls

The oldest stories and teachings in the Bible would have been retold for many generations. They were finally written down so they would not be forgotten. The first books were on rolled-up long sheets called scrolls. They were made from papyrus plants, written on with sooty ink. The scrolls were kept safe in clay jars.

The Dead Sea Scrolls were found rolled up inside storage jars with tight-fitting lids.

Q: What are the different types of writing?

There are different types of writing in the Bible. Here are some of the main ones.

History: These are factual stories reporting what happened at certain times and places, such as battles between the Jewish people and their enemies, and events in Jesus' life.

Laws: These are the rules that God gave to the Jewish people. They tell the people about the right and wrong way to live.

Poetry and wisdom: These include songs, or psalms (poems), to God, and wise sayings about how to live.

Prophecies: These are words of warning and promises, which are said to be messages from God. They include visions of the future and of heaven.

Letters: These are writings sent by some of the first followers of Jesus to teach and encourage one another to stay faithful to Jesus.

Joel was one of the prophets in the Old Testament.

7

Who wrote the BIBLE?

No one really knows exactly who many of **the writers** of the Bible are as the books were written so long ago. They were written in the **language** of the time by the people who lived in what is now the Middle East. Christians believe that all the writers of the Bible were helped and **inspired by God** to write the words.

Luke probably used writing materials like the ones on this desk.

The unknown writers

Some of the books are writings collected from different people and over time altered by others. Many of the books are named after a person, but that person may not have written them. They may have been written by their followers, such as the book of Isaiah. Others are named after a person whose story is told in the book, such as Jonah and Ruth. The letters could be named after the person they are from or are written to.

The known writers

Some of the writers of the New Testament books are known, such as Luke and Paul. They were both followers of Jesus soon after he lived and they journeyed with other Christians, spreading the message of Jesus to different countries. Luke wrote two books: one about Jesus, known as a gospel, and the other about what happened to the followers of Jesus, known as the book of Acts. Paul wrote in one of his letters:

All Scripture is inspired by God and is useful for teaching the truth, rebuking error, correcting faults, and giving instruction for right living, so that the person who serves God may be fully qualified and equipped to do every kind of good deed.

Q: What languages were used to write the Bible?

There are three languages used for writing the Bible.

Hebrew is the first language of the Jewish people and is used for most of the Old Testament.

Aramaic was the language of the Persian empire. The Jewish people changed to using this a few centuries before the time of Jesus. This is used in part of the book of Daniel. Jesus probably spoke Aramaic.

Greek was the language used through the Roman empire and is used for writing the New Testament. Christians wrote in Koine Greek, the everyday form that was easy to use, rather than the official form.

Did you KNOW?

The books in the Bible are not in the order of date that they were written.

Copy of Paul's letter on papyrus.

What is the OLD TESTAMENT?

Christians call the first and longer part of the Bible the **Old Testament**. The books were written and collected in the thousand years before the time of Jesus. They are from the Hebrew Bible, the holy book of the Jewish people, but have been grouped differently. The word "testament" means "agreement" or "**covenant**".

Law books:

Genesis | Exodus | Leviticus | Numbers | Deuteronomy

History books:

Joshua | Judges | Ruth | 1 Samuel | 2 Samuel | 1 Kings | 2 Kings | 1 Chronicles | 2 Chronicles | Ezra | Nehemiah | Esther

Books of Wisdom:

Job | Psalms | Proverbs | Ecclesiastes | Song of Solomon

Books of the Prophets:

Isaiah | Jeremiah | Lamentations | Ezekiel | Daniel | Hosea | Joel | Amos | Obadiah | Jonah | Micah | Nahum | Habakkuk | Zephaniah | Haggai | Zechariah | Malachi

The Old Testament books in the order they appear in the Bible.

Books of the Old Testament

The books of the Old Testament are grouped together. They begin with the law books, then the history books, followed by the books of Wisdom and lastly the books of the prophets.

Covenant

The Old Testament is called this because the books tell of God's agreement, or covenant, with the Jewish people. The books tell of the three great covenants that God made with Noah, then Abraham, and then with Moses. These were promises.

Q: What are the three great covenants?

The covenant, or promise, that God gave Noah was made after God had kept Noah, his family, and the animals safe from a flood. They had been in a huge floating boat, called the ark. God promised that never again will a flood destroy all living things on earth. A rainbow was the sign of God's covenant.

Also, in the book of Genesis is God's covenant with a man named Abraham. God promised to make him the father of a great nation, who would bring God's blessing to all the world. God showed Abraham the night sky, promising he would have more descendants than there were stars.

The covenant that God made with a great leader named Moses is found in the book of Exodus. The agreement was that the people would live by God's laws, then God promised to be their God and they would be God's people. God's laws, known as the Ten Commandments, were written on stone tablets, and kept in a golden box, called the Ark of the Covenant.

Did you KNOW?

Nobody knows what happened to the Ark of the Covenant. The hope that one day the Ark might be discovered is found in many movies and stories.

Two golden cherubim (angels) rested on the lid of the Ark of the Covenant.

How does the BIBLE begin?

The first five books of the Old Testament are known as the **law books**, but they are not just rules. The books are full of some of the **best-known stories** in the Bible. The stories set up the **special relationship** between God and people.

The creation story reminds readers that the world is God's, and the world was made good.

The law books

The first five books are Genesis, Exodus, Leviticus, Numbers, and Deuteronomy. They are known as the Pentateuch, or Torah, by the Jewish people. The Bible begins with a poem about God making the world in six days and resting on the seventh. The stories end with Moses leading God's people to the borders of the land they believed God promised them.

Best-known stories

The second story in the Bible is about God creating a garden paradise in Eden and making a man and a woman, Adam and Eve. They disobeyed God by eating the fruit of the Tree of the Knowledge of good and evil, spoiling the relationship between God and people. Other stories are about the members of the first family of God's chosen people and how their descendants were slaves in Egypt and God rescued them.

Q: What is God's special relationship with people?

On day six of the creation poem, God made people and saw that everything was very good. People were to oversee the care and responsibility of God's world.

In the Garden of Eden, God walked with the first man and the first woman. When they disobeyed God, they had to leave the garden and being close to God. This is called the Fall.

God chose a man named Abraham to begin the special relationship again. God promised him many descendants and the land of Canaan as a homeland.

Abraham's son Isaac had two sons, Esau and Jacob. Jacob, renamed Israel, had twelve sons who became heads of twelve different tribes, the beginning of God's chosen nation, to share God's blessing with the world.

The descendants of Israel were slaves in Egypt, but God helped Moses to lead them to freedom and back towards the promised land of Canaan. God's laws about how to live the right way were given to the people.

The arrows show Abraham's travels to the land of Canaan by the Mediterranean Sea.

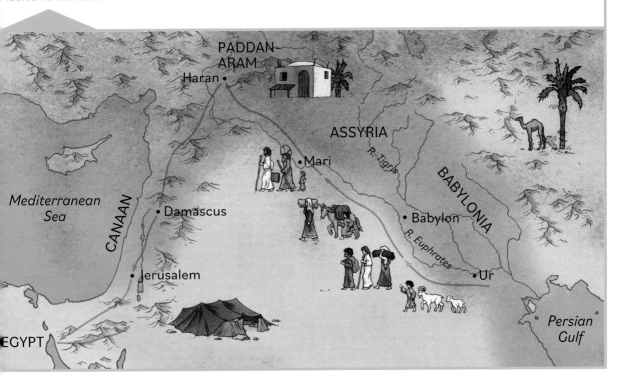

Are there LAWS in the law books?

The first five books of the Bible do contain the laws said to be given to **Moses at Mount Sinai** by God. The Jewish people say there are 613 altogether, but there are ten great laws known as the **Ten Commandments**. God's instructions also include making a **special tent of worship**.

Moses holding the stone tablets showing the Ten Commandments

Moses at Mount Sinai

The story of Moses in the book of Exodus tells how God's laws were given to the people through him. He went to the top of Mount Sinai, between Egypt and Canaan. Surrounded by thunder and lightning, Moses was told the right way to worship God and the right way that the people should treat one another.

Did you KNOW?

Jesus was a Jew and followed the laws, but he criticized some religious leaders, who showed off how religious they were and wanted to be admired.

The Ten Commandments

These ten great laws sum up all the laws and were carved onto stone tablets.

1. I am the Lord your God, who brought you out of Egypt, where you were slaves. Worship no god but me.
2. Do not make for yourselves images of anything in heaven or on earth, or in the water under the earth. Do not bow down to any idol or worship it.
3. Do not use my name for evil purposes.
4. Observe the Sabbath and keep it holy.
5. Respect your father and mother.
6. Do not commit murder.
7. Do not commit adultery.
8. Do not steal.
9. Do not accuse anyone falsely.
10. Do not desire what belongs to another.

Q: What was the special tent for God?

When God gave Moses the ten great laws, the people were on a journey and living in tents. God told Moses exactly how to make a special tent for worshipping God and the objects that were needed. This was called the tabernacle.

There was a seven-branched lamp called the menorah, which always stayed lit as a sign of God's presence with them. Hidden behind the curtains was kept the golden Ark of the Covenant as a symbol of God with them.

Priests burnt ~erings to God on ~ altar in front of ~he tabernacle.

The next twelve books in the Old Testament are the **history books**. They tell the history of the Israelite people from the time of Moses onwards. They include stories about great heroes, or **judges**, and then their decision to be ruled by a **king**.

The history books

The first five history books are Joshua, Judges, Ruth, 1 Samuel, and 2 Samuel. Joshua was the name of the leader after Moses. He led the people into the land of Canaan and helped them to settle there. The book of Judges tells of the times when the people were attacked by other nations. The book of Ruth was set during this time.

The first kings

The books of Samuel are about the last of the judges and the first kings. As a boy, Samuel was a helper at a holy shrine. He became greatly respected as able to settle quarrels and guide people how to live as God wanted. When the people asked for a king to lead them, Samuel listened to God and anointed Saul and then a shepherd boy, David. When David became king, he captured the city of Jerusalem.

When Joshua led the people into Canaan, they first had to capture the walled city of Jericho. God told Joshua what to do. On the seventh day of marching around Jericho, the priests blew their trumpets, the people shouted, and the city walls crumbled.

Q: Who were some of the judges?

The land of Canaan was divided among the twelve tribes of the people. At times, the people turned away from God. When they were attacked by their enemies, they believe God chose leaders to save them.

Othniel was the first judge and, after a war, the people lived at peace for forty years.

Ehud was the left-handed judge who killed the Moabite king, who ruled over the people. After defeating the Moab army, the people lived at peace for eighty years.

Deborah was a prophetess, who sat under a palm tree and people went to her for advice. She told a warrior, Barak, to fight the Canaanite army led by Sisera. She went with him and the army was defeated.

Gideon was a reluctant judge but guided by God – and with an army of just 300 men – he defeated the huge Midianite army.

Samson was a strong man, and God used his strength to defeat the Philistines, who had taken over the land.

Did you KNOW?

Ruth was from Moab, but she went with her Israelite mother-in-law to Bethlehem. Ruth married a landowner, Boaz. She was the great grandmother of David. Ruth promised: *Your people will be my people and your God will be my God.*

Gideon's army just used burning torches and trumpets to confuse and defeat the Midianites.

WHAT HAPPENS NEXT in the history books?

The seven other history books are
1 Kings, 2 Kings, 1 Chronicles, 2
Chronicles, Ezra, Nehemiah, and
Esther. These books tell the story of
how **the kingdom became divided**,
the Israelites turned away from God
and were conquered, and the people
were scattered. Eventually they
returned to **rebuild Jerusalem**.

A divided kingdom

King David was succeeded by one of his sons,
Solomon. Solomon was famous for his wisdom
and Israel's kingdom became powerful. After
his death, there was a quarrel about who
should be the next king. The kingdom was
divided. The northern kingdom of Israel was
ruled by kings, who did not respect God.
The southern kingdom of Judah was ruled by
Solomon's descendants, who also forgot God.

Conquered

The kingdom of Israel was destroyed by the
Assyrians in 722 BCE. A few hundred years
later, the kingdom of Judah was defeated by
the Babylonians. The people were taken to live
in other parts of the empire and the city of
Jerusalem was destroyed. When the Persians
took control of the Babylonian empire, the
people of Judah, now called Jews, were allowed
back to Jerusalem. Nehemiah took charge of
rebuilding the walls.

*When the two
kingdoms were
divided, the capital
of Judah was
Jerusalem, and the
capital of Israel
was Shechem.*

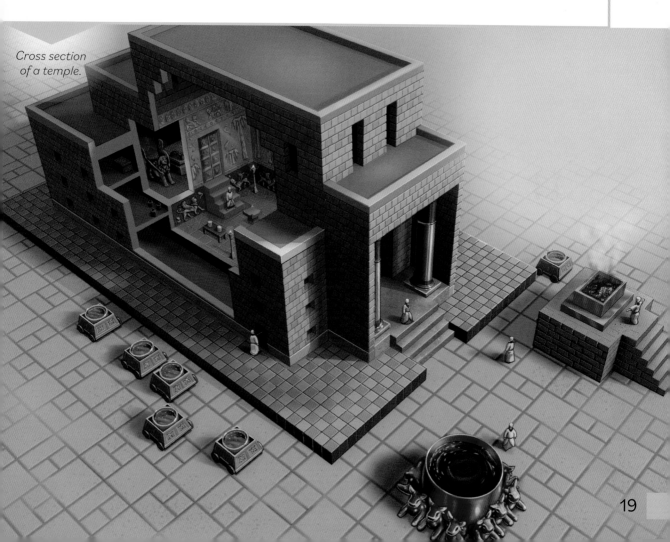

Did you KNOW?

Esther was a Jewish woman, who was chosen by the Persian emperor to be his queen. With great courage, she saved the Jewish people from a plot to kill them all. Esther was told: *Yet who knows - maybe it was for a time like this that you were made queen!*

Q: Who built the temple in Jerusalem?

The first book of Kings describes how Solomon built the first temple in Jerusalem. This became the main place for the people to worship God and the Ark of the Covenant was placed here behind a curtain. The insides were covered in gold. Solomon's temple was destroyed by the Babylonians, all the treasures were taken, and the Ark was never seen again. When the Jewish people returned, a priest named Ezra took charge of building the new temple and this is told in the book of Ezra.

Cross section of a temple.

What are the books of WISDOM?

There are five so-called books of Wisdom in the Old Testament: Job, Psalms, Proverbs, Ecclesiastes, and The Song of Solomon. Each book has a very different style of writing, from **drama, songs, and love poems** to asking **questions** that are answered with **wise advice**.

Drama, songs, and love poems

The book of Job is a drama about a good man who suffers all kinds of horrible things, and wonders what God thinks and does about suffering. The book of Psalms is a hymn book of prayers, songs, and poems, still used by Jewish and Christian people. King David is said to have written many of them. The Song of Solomon is a collection of love poems.

Did you KNOW?

The book of Job is thought to be the oldest book in the Bible, as he probably lived at the same time as Abraham.

At the start of his story, Job was a wealthy man. Despite losing everything, he still loved God.

Questions and wise words

The book of Ecclesiastes asks all kinds of questions about life. The book explores what life would be like without God and then how meaning in life comes from enjoying the everyday with God. The book of Proverbs is full of wise sayings to help people lead good lives. These include: *Kind words are like honey – sweet to the taste and good for your health.*

Honey is used many times in the Bible to mean sweetness, wisdom, and abundance.

Q: What are some of the famous psalms?

The book of Psalms is, after Jeremiah and Genesis, the third longest book of the Bible and has 150 different psalms. The word "praise" appears 211 times.

Psalm 19 praises the work and words of God. It begins: *How clearly the sky reveals God's glory! How plainly it shows what he has done!*

Psalm 23 begins: *The Lord is my shepherd*. Many people think this was written by King David, who was a shepherd boy when young.

Psalm 100 is about thanks and praise to God and begins: *Shout for joy to the Lord, all the earth.*

Psalm 117 is the shortest psalm, with just two verses.

Psalm 118: There are 594 chapters in the Bible before and after this psalm, which totals 1188. The very middle of the Bible is Psalm 118 verse 8: *It is better to trust in the Lord than to depend on people.*

Psalm 119 is the longest psalm. Each of the twenty-two sections begins with a different letter of the Hebrew alphabet. It praises God's Law: *Your word is a lamp to guide me and a light for my path.*

King David was a gifted musician.

Who were the PROPHETS?

The seventeen **books of the prophets** are about the people who spoke to others about the messages they had received from God. These prophets gave **warnings** and **messages of hope** to the people of their time. The books are not in the **timeline order** that they were written, but the longer books come first.

Books of the prophets

The five longest books are called the "major prophets": Isaiah, Jeremiah, Lamentations, Ezekiel, and Daniel. The shorter books are called the "minor prophets": Hosea, Joel, Amos, Obadiah, Jonah, Micah, Nahum, Habakkuk, Zephaniah, Haggai, Zechariah, and Malachi. Many are written as if the prophets are speaking, but they were probably written by the followers of the prophets.

Warnings and forgiveness

The people in the northern kingdom of Israel and the southern kingdom of Judah often forgot God's law. The prophets warned them to obey God, otherwise all that they have would be taken away, and they would be defeated by their enemies. The story of Jonah shows that God was ready to forgive even their enemies, the Assyrians, if people turned away from their wicked ways.

Jeremiah was one of the prophets and is sometimes called "the weeping prophet" because he was sad about what would happen to his people.

Messages of hope

When the people were defeated and their kings killed, the prophets began to speak of a king sent by God, who would change everything. The word for God's chosen king was "Messiah". Christians believe that Jesus was the Messiah. The prophet Isaiah said:

The people who walked in darkness have seen a great light. They lived in a land of shadows, but now light is shining on them... A son is given to us! And he will be our ruler. He will be called, "Wonderful Counsellor", "Mighty God", "Eternal Father", "Prince of Peace".

Did you KNOW?

The prophets were from different backgrounds. Isaiah belonged to a royal family, while Amos and Micah were farmers.

Q: What was the timeline of the prophets?

1. Amos and Hosea warned the people in Israel. They did not listen. The Assyrians conquered them.
2. Isaiah and Micah warned the people in Judah that Assyria would defeat them.
3. Jonah warned the Assyrians, but Nahum rejoices when they were defeated by the Babylonians.
4. Jeremiah, Zephaniah, and Habakkuk warned that the Babylonians would defeat Judah.
5. The writer of Lamentations and Obadiah mourned the defeat of Jerusalem in Judah.
6. Ezekiel, Daniel, and the second part of Isaiah brought hope to the people who had been taken to Babylon.
7. Haggai, Zechariah, and Malachi brought hope to the people returning to Jerusalem.

Where and when the prophet Joel lived is uncertain.

THE PROPHETS IN THEIR TIME

3 • Nineveh

6

4 • Babylon

1
• Samaria

Jerusalem •
2   5
         7

The numbers show the places connected with the prophets.

Some Christian Bibles have more books in the Old Testament than others. The Jews collected all their important writings, and these were carefully translated into Greek. This work is known as the **Septuagint**. These include extra writings than in the Hebrew Bible, which are called the **Apocrypha**.

Often one scribe read the text aloud, while others made copies, and other scribes checked.

The Septuagint

A few hundred years before the time of Jesus, there were Jews living in different parts of the Greek empire. Each community wanted a collection of the scriptures that had been collected over many hundreds of years. They understood Greek more than Hebrew, so seventy scholars translated the writings and carefully made copies for them. This work is known as the Septuagint, from the Latin word for seventy.

Did you KNOW?

Bel and the dragon is the story of the Jewish prophet Daniel, who is thrown into a den of lions, after refusing to worship the god Bel and killing the dragon. After seven days, Daniel leaves unharmed.

The Apocrypha

The first Christians used the Septuagint, and this makes up the Old Testament used by Roman Catholic Christians today. When the Jews finally chose the special writings for their Hebrew Bible, they considered some books not important enough to include. About 500 years ago, Protestant Christians decided that the shorter collection was better for their Old Testament. The extra books are called the Apocrypha or Deuterocanonical books.

List of the Deuterocanonical books

Note: They are not all included in all Bibles, especially the ones in brackets.

Tobit
Judith
Additions to Esther
Wisdom of Solomon
Sirach (also called Ecclesiasticus)
Baruch
Letter of Jeremiah
Prayer of Azariah and the
 Song of the three young men
Susanna
Bel and the dragon
1 Maccabees
2 Maccabees
(3 Maccabees)
(4 Maccabees)
1 Esdras
2 Esdras
Prayer of Manasseh

Q: Who were the Maccabees?

Judas Maccabeus lived in the time when the Greeks had conquered the land of the Jews. The Greeks had even put statues of Greek gods in the Jewish temple in Jerusalem. Judas and his brothers, who were Jewish priests, led a rebellion to remove these statues from the temple and rededicated it to God. Jews celebrate this event at the festival of Hanukkah in December each year.

The Maccabees take back the ruined temple from the Greeks.

What is the NEW TESTAMENT?

The **New Testament** continues from the stories of God's special relationship with the Jewish people. Christians believe that Jesus was **Christ**, God's special king, hoped for in the Old Testament. They believe God's son came to live on earth and makes a **new covenant**, or agreement, with **all people**.

Gospels:

Matthew · Mark · Luke · John · Acts of the Apostles

Letters:

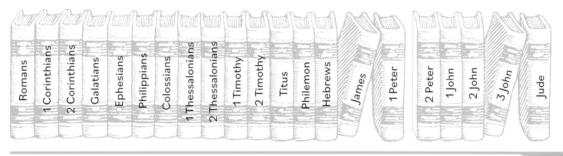

Romans · 1 Corinthians · 2 Corinthians · Galatians · Ephesians · Philippians · Colossians · 1 Thessalonians · 2 Thessalonians · 1 Timothy · 2 Timothy · Titus · Philemon · Hebrews · James · 1 Peter · 2 Peter · 1 John · 2 John · 3 John · Jude · Revelation

Books of the New Testament

The New Testament begins with four accounts that tell the story of Jesus' life, death, and resurrection, known as the four Gospels. The Acts of the Apostles tells how Jesus' followers spread the news about him through the world. Then follows the letters by a man named Paul and other new Christians. The final book is by a man named John and details a vision of a new heaven and a new earth.

Christ the king

The writers of the New Testament show how Jesus was descended from King David, the most famous king in the Old Testament. They also believed that he was Christ the special king, or Messiah, sent by God to rescue and restore the people with God as spoken about by various prophets.

Books of the New Testament in the order that they appear in the Bible.

Q: What is the new covenant?

Christians believe that after Jesus died, he was raised to life, or resurrected. They believe that, through his death, Jesus opened the way back to God. He restored the relationship between God and all people that was broken when Adam and Eve disobeyed God in the book of Genesis. This rescue plan is called salvation. The promise was made when Jesus shared his last meal with his disciples.

Then he took a piece of bread, gave thanks to God, broke it, and gave it to them [his disciples] saying, "This is my body, which is given for you. Do this in memory of me." In the same way, he gave them the cup after the supper, saying, "This cup is God's new covenant sealed with my blood, which is poured out for you."

Did you KNOW?

Since the time of Jesus his followers have shared bread and wine together. They remember the agreement, believing that those who follow Jesus are welcomed into God's everlasting kingdom.

Jesus shared two signs with his followers: bread and wine.

What are the GOSPELS?

The first four books of the New Testament are called the **Gospels**. The first three gospels are Matthew, Mark, and Luke, and tell similar stories about **Jesus' life and teachings**. The fourth gospel, John, is written very differently, showing who Jesus is.

The Gospels

The word "gospel" means "good news". Christians believe that Jesus is God in the flesh, or incarnate, come to live among humans. Jesus was born a Jew. He lived and taught in his home region near the inland sea of Galilee. He was accused by the Jewish people of being a troublemaker and arrested in Jerusalem. The Roman rulers killed him as a criminal, nailing him to a cross of wood, known as crucifixion. Jesus body was laid in a tomb by his friends. Three days later he was seen again, and his friends witnessed that he was alive. Forty days later, Jesus was lifted to heaven.

Jesus' teachings

The Gospels tell about how Jesus came to show and teach what it means to be loved by God and belong to the kingdom of God. He told stories, called parables, to the crowds who gathered around him. These parables helped people to understand more about God, such as God's love and forgiveness, and how to live in God's kingdom following Jesus' example.

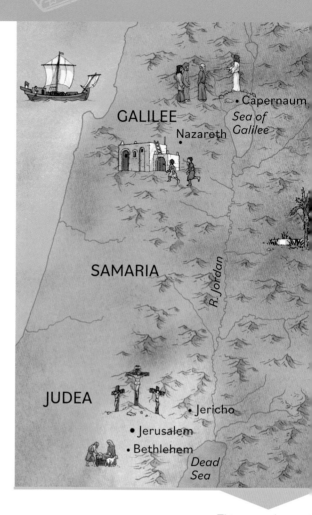

This map shows the places where Jesus went in the Gospels.

Jesus told the parable of a shepherd who had 100 sheep. When one was lost, he searched and brought it safely home. The shepherd was so happy that he had a party. This described how God as shepherd looks after people.

Q: Why is the crucifixion important?

Christians believe that Jesus loved them so much that he was willing to die for them although he had done nothing wrong himself. Through his death they get forgiven for all the bad things they do and become friends with God again. They believe that Jesus' resurrection proves that there is life after death and gives hope. Christians remember these events at Easter.

One Easter tradition is to make a tiny Easter garden showing three crosses on a hillside and the empty tomb to remember Jesus' death and resurrection.

What do we know about JESUS?

The stories of Jesus say that he was born in Bethlehem, the birthplace of King David. He grew up in Nazareth and then began preaching and showing wondrous signs, or **miracles**. He talked about what was important in God's law, giving a **new commandment** about love, and teaching people how to pray, known as the **Lord's prayer**.

A boy offers Jesus his basket of two fish and five loaves.

Miracles

In the Gospels, there are stories about how Jesus gave many signs, or miracles, which showed that he had the power of God. There were different types of miracles. Jesus blessed a boy's lunch of five loaves and two fish, which then fed a huge crowd with some left over. He healed many sick people with just a touch and even raised a girl and his friend from the dead. One story was about Jesus calming a storm just by telling the wind to be quiet.

A new commandment

A Jewish teacher of the Law asked Jesus which of the Ten Commandments was the greatest and Jesus summed them up, replying: *The Lord our God is the only Lord. Love the Lord your God with all your heart and with all your soul and with all your strength and with all your mind* and *Love others as yourself*. Jesus also gave his followers a new commandment to live by: *As I have loved you, so you must love one another*.

Did you KNOW?

The Jewish historian Josephus mentions Jesus in his accounts and says he did miracles and was crucified.

Jesus teaches his followers on the hillsides around the Sea of Galilee.

Q: What is the Lord's prayer?

Jesus' friends asked him to help them to talk with God in prayer. The prayer that Jesus taught them is still used by Christians all over the world.

Our Father in heaven,
May your holy name be honoured;
may your Kingdom come;
may your will be done on earth as it is in heaven.
Give us today the food we need.
Forgive us the wrongs we have done,
as we forgive the wrongs that others have done to us.
Do not bring us to hard testing,
but keep us safe from the Evil One.

WHAT HAPPENED after Jesus?

The fifth book of the New Testament is called the **Acts of the Apostles**. The book begins with the Holy Spirit of God coming and giving Jesus' followers courage and wisdom to continue to spread the **good news** message to all people. The book tells how they shared his message with others (Jews and non-Jews), the challenges they faced, and the people they met, who converted to following Jesus.

The apostles John and Peter were important in founding the church, those who believed in Jesus Christ.

The Acts of the Apostles

The book was written by the gospel writer Luke, who was a doctor and was interested in miracles. He begins the book with these words:

Dear Theophilus
In my first book I wrote about all the things that Jesus did and taught from the time he began his work until the day he was taken up to heaven. Before he was taken up, he gave instructions by the power of the Holy Spirit to the men he had chosen as his apostles.

The apostles

The word "apostle" means "one who is sent" and was the name given to the group of followers chosen by Jesus. Despite the threat to their lives, they spoke out bravely about Jesus and belonging to the kingdom of God. As a sign of becoming a follower of Jesus, the apostles baptized people, by pouring water over them. The apostles, such as Peter, were also able to heal people with just a touch.

Did you KNOW?

One of the people persecuting the Christians was a Jewish leader, or Pharisee, named Saul. On the road to Damascus he heard Jesus speaking to him. He was converted to being a follower, changed his name to Paul, and spent the rest of his life helping spread the news.

Q: How did the good news about Jesus spread?

The apostles began preaching in Jerusalem, but some of the religious leaders became angry. One of the new followers of Christ was Stephen. He was stoned to death for speaking about Jesus as the promised king, alive and reigning in heaven. The apostles scattered, but this meant they reached more people to talk about how their sins were forgiven through Jesus. The apostle Philip explained the good news to an Ethiopian.

The meeting of the apostle Philip with an Ethiopian man is told in the Acts of the Apostles.

How did Christians STAY IN TOUCH?

Much of the Acts of the Apostles tells about the **journeys** of a man named Paul, who spread the news about Jesus to non-Jews, or

ITALY
Rome
Puteoli
Syracuse
MALTA
GREECE
Philippi
Thessalonica
Corinth
Athens
ASIA
Ephesus
Colossae
Chidus
Myra
GALATIA
Anti
CRETE
Salmone
CYPRUS
S
Ca
Mediterranean Sea

Gentiles. Soon there were groups of Christians, or churches, in different cities around the Mediterranean Sea. Paul and other early Christians wrote **letters** to these first churches to encourage and guide them.

The map shows the many places that Paul visited on his journeys, and the route of his last journey to Rome.

Paul's journeys

Paul took the message about Jesus into Europe. After journeying through what is now Turkey, he went into Greece. In the end, Paul was arrested because Christianity was not allowed in the Roman empire at that time. He was sent to Rome for trial, where he was imprisoned in a house where he lived. He dictated some letters to a scribe from there.

Paul's letters

Paul wrote many letters to the Christian groups, or churches, he had helped to set up. There are thirteen in the Bible: Romans, 1 and 2 Corinthians, Galatians, Ephesians, Philippians, Colossians, 1 and 2 Thessalonians, 1 and 2 Timothy, Titus, and Philemon. The letters are named after the people to whom they were sent, such as the Christians in Rome, and his friend Timothy.

Q: What was in the letters in the Bible?

The letters encouraged the first groups of Jesus' followers in their faith. They were encouraged not to give up, even if they were facing a hard time from others. They answered questions about what Christians believed. They helped to settle disagreements between people. They gave advice about how to live and to church leaders.

The runaway slave Onesimus gives Paul's letter to his master Philemon. Paul asks Philemon to forgive Onesimus, who has become a believer in Jesus.

In one of Paul's letters to the church in Corinth, he summed up all his advice, writing:

Strive for perfection; listen to my appeals; agree with one another; live in peace. And the God of love and peace will be with you... The grace of the Lord Jesus Christ, the love of God, and the fellowship of the Holy Spirit be with you all.

Did you KNOW?

The other letters in the Bible are Hebrews, James, 1 Peter, 2 Peter, 1 John, 2 John, 3 John, and Jude. Despite the names, no one knows for sure who wrote them.

Does the Bible describe HEAVEN?

The last book of the New Testament is the **book of Revelation**. This was an **amazing vision** given to a man named John, who was imprisoned on the island of Patmos. The vision ends with a description of a **new heaven**.

The apostle John writes his vision, giving glimpses into the future.

The book of Revelation

John wrote that one day Jesus appeared before him, dazzling in glory, and he was told to send messages to seven churches. These were words of warning and of encouragement in times of trouble. Then John is shown heaven and the events that will lead to the end of times. The vision provides hope and encouragement for people in troubled times.

Amazing vision

After seeing the worship of God in heaven, John sees a vision of a great battle between good and evil. This ends with the final victory of God and God's goodness, and a day of judgement. Then there is a vision of a new heaven descending. An angel shows him this new Eden with streets paved with gold, a river of the water of life, and the tree of life.

Did you KNOW?

Many ideas about what heaven is like comes from the book of Revelation, such as the pearly gates, saints dressed in white, and a city of gold.

igh priest wearing breastplate with twelve precious stones.

Q: Why is the vision very mysterious?

John's vision is full of numbers and names of jewels. These are like a code, representing things that connect with significant events in the Bible, and have a symbolic meaning. For example, the number twelve links with the twelve tribes of Israel and the twelve apostles. The number twelve means "perfection". The garments of the priests in the time of Moses had twelve gemstones set in gold for each of the twelve tribes. John describes the new heaven:

The city's wall was built on twelve foundation stones, on which were written the names of the twelve apostles... The foundation stones of the city wall were adorned with all kinds of precious stones. The first foundation stone was jasper, the second sapphire, the third agate, the fourth emerald, the fifth onyx, the sixth carnelian, the seventh yellow quartz, the eighth beryl, the ninth topaz, the tenth chalcedony, the eleventh turquoise, the twelfth amethyst.

What is the HISTORY of the Bible?

There were many writings about Jesus, and selecting which books to include in a Bible was carefully considered. In 397, **the official Bible**, or canon, of scripture was decided in Carthage, north Africa by a council of bishops (church leaders). The Bible was **translated** first into Latin and, for many hundreds of years, hand-copied. But now it is printed in over 2,000 languages.

The official Bible

In 312, a Roman emperor named Constantine became a Christian and the faith became the official religion of the empire. At last Christians could meet openly, and the emperor was happy for them to spread the faith. Church leaders met and put the collection of the Christian writings of the New Testament, selected about 150 years after the time of Jesus, with the longer collection of Jewish writings.

Translations

In 384, the leader of the church, Pope Damascus, arranged for someone named Jerome to translate the Bible into Latin, the language of the Roman empire. This translation is called the Vulgate. For hundreds of years after, copies of this Bible were made, carefully written by hand. In the fifteenth century, people protested and wanted to read the Bible for themselves. Translations were made into the main European languages. As people began exploring other parts of the world, they spread the message of Christianity, and the Bible was translated into many different languages.

The books of the Old Testament and New Testament were copied by Christian monks.

Did you KNOW?

About 1456, soon after the invention of the printing press, one of the first books to be printed was a Bible in Latin.

n some Christian traditions, there is a special procession before the reading of the Gospel.

Q: Who reads the Bible?

All over the world today, Christians read the Bible. The Bible is read aloud in church services daily and weekly. Many Christians like to have a Bible of their own. Some read it every day. Others may read it occasionally to find words of help or wisdom. Some Christians meet to read and study the Bible.

The Bible contains many words, and it can seem quite difficult to know where to begin. Most modern Bibles are organized in a helpful way with **chapters and verses**. The Bible is not just a book, and many important stories or events are **illustrated** in churches.

Chapters and verses

At the front of a Bible is a list of the books, which provides a page number. Often the New Testament starts again on page 1. Within each book, there are larger numbers that mark the chapters. Within the words, there are tiny numbers, which are the numbers of the verses. People use the name of the book, the chapter, and the verse to help find the part they are looking for.

Large chapter number

LUKE 11

11 One day Jesus was praying in a certain place. When he had finished, one of his disciples said to him, 'Lord, teach us to pray, just as John taught his disciples.'
2 Jesus said to them, 'When you pray, say this:
"Father:
May your holy name be honoured;
may your Kingdom come.
3 Give us day by day the food we need.
4 Forgive us our sins,
for we forgive everyone who
does us wrong.
And do not bring us to
hard testing."'

Name of
book and
number c
the chapt
on this pa

Verse numbers

The opening verses of the Gospel of Luke, chapter 11.

Illustrated Bible stories

In the past many people were unable to read. They had to listen to a priest read from the Bible to get to know the stories. Many of the stories were brought to life for them through the paintings and stained-glass windows in churches.

Apostles in a boat is shown in a stained glass church window.

Did you KNOW?

The Bible was separated into chapters in the thirteenth century. It was split into verses in the sixteenth century.

Q: Where are some stories in the Bible?

The story of **Noah** is in the book of Genesis. It starts at chapter 6, verse 9 and ends at chapter 9, verse 17. This may be shown as Gen 6:9–9:17.

The story of **David** fighting the huge soldier, Goliath, is in the book of 1 Samuel. It starts at chapter 17, verse 1 and ends at verse 51. This may be shown as 1 Sam 17:1–51.

The story of **feeding 5,000** people is found in four different places. One of these is the Gospel of Mark, starting at chapter 6, verse 30 and ending at verse 44. This may be shown as Mark 6:30–44.

The parable of the **Good Samaritan** is found in the Gospel of Luke, chapter 10, verses 25 to 37. This may be shown as Luke 10:25–37.

Noah, his family, and the animals leave the ark after the flood.

What is the Bible's MESSAGE?

Although the Bible was written a long time ago, Christians believe the book is helpful for their lives today. People read the Bible to find out more **about God** and **how God wants people to live**. Sometimes people read to find out what to do in a particular situation and learn new things from it all the time.

The cross is a symbol of the Christian faith.

About God

Throughout the Bible stories, the writers show God's love for people. The writers of the New Testament believe that Jesus coming to earth was the greatest sign of God's love. The first Christians speak of how Jesus overcame death to bring eternal life. They wrote about this hope through faith in Jesus, believing they will be safe with God for ever.

About how to live

The Bible tells stories about God making the world and so people should care and look after all living things. They tell of God caring about how people treat one another and wanting people to live peacefully and fairly with one another. There are stories about people failing to do the right thing, but the prophets and Jesus talk about God's forgiveness, and so people should forgive one another. Jesus also came with a message that people should love God and one another and he welcomed everyone to be part of "God's kingdom".

Q: How is the Bible's message spread?

The Bible records that the final words of Jesus to his followers was to go out and tell others. Christians through the centuries have travelled the world, passing on the news about Jesus and his teaching found in the Bible.

This map shows the areas where Christianity is an important religion.

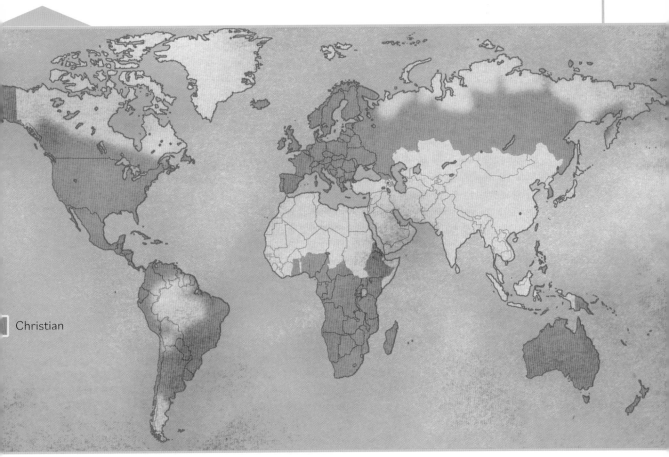

Christian

GLOSSARY

Apostle: Jesus' chosen followers sent to tell others about the faith.

Baptism: A ceremony when someone is dipped into holy water or it is sprinkled on their head to symbolize belonging to the Christian church.

Canon: The agreed list of books in the Bible.

Christ: A title based on a Greek word that means "chosen king".

Commandments: Special laws given to Moses by God.

Covenant: An agreement made between God and the people.

Deuterocanon: A second list of books included in some Bibles.

Disciple: Someone who learns from a teacher, a follower of Jesus.

Idol: A statue that is worshipped.

Incarnation: God in human form.

Israel: The name of the people descended from Abraham, Isaac, and Jacob (also called Israel). The people of Israel were also called Hebrews or, later, Jews.

Judge: A person chosen to decide or advise on quarrels or take a lead guided by God.

Messiah: A title based on a Hebrew word that means "promised king", who will save people.

Pentateuch: The first five books of the Old Testament.

Prophet: Someone who receives messages from God and passes them on to the people.

Proverb: A wise saying that has a deeper meaning.

Psalms: Songs to God.

Resurrection: The name for Jesus being raised from the dead.

Sabbath: A holy day of rest and focus on God.

Salvation: The rescue plan of God to bring people back to be with God.

Scroll: A long document that can be rolled and unrolled.

Temple: A building for the worship of God.

Testament: An agreement or covenant.

Vision: Something seen in a dream or trance.

Worship: The act of praise, prayer, and giving thanks to God.

BIBLE REFERENCES

All references are taken from the Good News Bible.

A young David slings a rock at the Philistine champion warrior, Goliath.

INDEX